AF578743

Why Not Me?

ARE YOU TIRED OF BEING JUST AMONG THE OTHERS BUT NEVER BEING THE ONE?

STEPHEN MUIRU

creativeeve
Create · Design · Style

Why Not Me?

Copyright © 2016 Stephen Muiru
All rights reserved

Published in Kenya by Creative-eve
Copyright © 2016 Creative-eve.
Email: maggie.munyua@gmail.com **Cell:** +254726210515
All rights reserved.

No part of this publication may be reproduced, stored in a retrieval system or transmitted in any form or by any means electronic, mechanical, photocopying, recording or otherwise, without the prior written permission of the author except as provided by copyright law.

This book is designed to provide accurate and authoritative information with regard to the subject matter covered. It is here with the understanding that the publisher and the contributors are not engaged in rendering legal, accounting or other professional advice. If legal or other professional assistance is required, the services of a competent professional should be sought. The reader is advised to consult with an appropriately qualified professional before making any business decision.

ISBN: 978-9966-790-46-0

DEDICATION

To God Be the Glory!

1. To my lovely wife Judy, sons Ronald and Gregory and daughter Lisa for your unconditional love and encouragement.

2. In a very special way to my father: You have been bravely fighting cancer and other related complications for the last ten years. You have demonstrated tremendous courage and you have been a real source of inspiration for me.

3. Mum for your unfailing love.

4. My brothers and sisters for being the best siblings I could ever ask for.

5. Lastly to my late brother and best friend Rufus, and my late sister Zipporah. May your souls rest in eternal peace.

Acknowledgements

1. Pepe Minambo, renowned author, international motivational speaker and my coach at the Pepe Minambo Motivational Speaking Academy for introducing me to myself and encouraging me to write this book.

2. All the students who recently graduated from the Pepe Minambo Motivational Speaking Academy for your support and dedication to transform Kenya, Africa and the world.

3. All of you who allowed me to use your life stories in this book. I say thank you so much.

4. To Maggie Munyua, CEO Creative Eve Publishers for your artistic design and layout. For her passionate will that it can be done. Thank you for agreeing to publish my first book ever.

5. My wonderful editing team for your wonderful work on my maiden book.

CONTENTS

INTRODUCTION

Do you know that you are a vessel; a divine vessel for that matter? Every human being is a vessel put here on earth by God for a divine purpose. Unfortunately, nobody is born with an operating manual and therefore, one has to figure out on their own what their real purpose here on earth is.

I have been a practitioner in the field of architecture for the last twenty years. I have literally written poetry in stone and mortar. In that time, I have had the privilege of designing and supervising a project sponsored by the government of Kenya with the blessings of former president Mwai Kibaki among many other projects. I was the architect and manager for the 'Change the Face of Mang'u High School' project between 2009 and 2012, which comprised of, an ultra-modern amphitheater, a state of the art administration block, new classes, laboratories and dormitory block. This, by any stretch of imagination was no mean feat. Just to have ones designs presented to the president is a dream for any architect! To have the president consent to the designs was a dream come-true for me! Supervising the implementation of the project to completion and seeing the reality of my creativity was just surreal!

I always say an architect should be very thankful when a client implements his design because that gives the architect's design visibility. Now imagine what it means when your project is the signature of Mang'u High School? A project that has the approval of the president, no less! That to me is like getting free advertisement space on the front page of Daily Nation, the biggest daily in Kenya, for the rest of my life!

The strange thing is that even after handling that project and all the others in my twenty years of practice, I still had an emptiness I could not explain. Many were the times I asked God; "*If other people who were doing smaller projects seemed happy, Why Not Me?*" This continued bothering me since as well as a thriving career, I am also blessed with a lovely family that I adore and a wonderful network of friends.

The reality is that many live without realizing their purpose in life. They live like cars trying to drive on the ocean or ships trying to move on land. The result being, the car will wonder why it is sinking, while the ship moves effortlessly on water. The ship will wonder why it never makes a step forward, while the car whistles its way as it glides on land. Other people are like vessels operating at partial capacity. Can you imagine a Ferrari with an eight gear transmission engine system but never goes beyond gear four? The car will never reach peak performance. I realized the void in me was because I was operating like such a car. Something was holding me back.

Charlie 'Tremendous' Jones once said, *"You will be the same person in five years as you are today except for the people you meet and the books you read."* A face book friend whom I had never met by the name Renee posted something very inspirational on her page. After reading it, the spirit of the Lord spoke to me and directed me to seek an appointment with her. When the spirit speaks you better listen! I sent her a message and she agreed to meet me. She was attending Pepe Minambo Motivational Speaking Academy to learn how to inspire people. The strange thing is I had invited Pepe Minambo in February 2015, four months before meeting Renee, to come and give a motivational talk to form fours in Mang'u High School. At that time he did not have an academy. I remember after the talk I had a chat with him and he told me he thought I had the gift of being a motivational speaker. At that time I dismissed it. Now here I was listening to Renee telling me about his Motivational Speaking Academy. Renee convinced me to join the academy. I called Pepe immediately and I signed up for his next class.

What I did not know was that through Pepe's coaching, I would discover the emptiness in me was because I had not met me! Pepe Minambo introduced me to myself. How about that! He made me realize I was like the Ferrari operating at half capacity. He made me realize that I had self-imposed limitations. He inspired me to get out of my comfort zone and go beyond limits!

The 'Me' I met came with a divine master key to the hidden treasures within me. That included inspiration to write this book, "Why Not Me?" Through this book I seek to share lessons I have learnt through my life experiences, some of which were replayed to me as flashes when I had a near fatal accident on 29th June, 2009. Others are lessons I have learnt through other people's experiences. All of them are vital lessons for us to help answer the question, "Why Not Me?"

#1

THE LIFE CHANGING ACCIDENT!

On 29th June, 2009, I had a near death experience. I was driving to Kakamega for a project I was doing for an insurance company. My journey had started from Nairobi at 11:00am. I was with a colleague, Ken, who was helping me with the project. As we approached Naivasha town, we had a puncture and we pulled over at a petrol station to have it repaired. We decided to take advantage of our forced break to have lunch. My colleague is a fine artist and I am an architect. We have utmost respect for each other and we often meet and chat about our newest projects and have interesting conversations down memory lane of art and architecture.

"No one can ever erase the legacy you leave once you know you gave it your all."

As we had lunch, we discussed tragic stories of great artists who died poor despite their great art pieces but have gone on to make obscene amounts of money posthumously through the sale of the same pieces by some art dealers. I remember telling my colleague that I hoped his art pieces would start selling well while he was still alive so that he may enjoy the fruits of his creativity. Ken said something very profound that I will never forget. He said that real happiness is not in the money but in pursuing your purpose with passion. Once you do that, the money will follow and even overtake you.

He added that, the greatest reward that you can get from your work is the joy of knowing you have given it your very best. He said he gets on a real high whenever he empties himself into his art work! "No one can ever erase the

> *'Live full, die empty.'*
>
> **-DR. MYLES MUNROE**

legacy you leave once you know you gave it your all." How true this is! It reminds me of Dr. Myles Munroe's famous saying, ***'Live full, die empty.'***

We set off on our journey and got to Nakuru. It started raining heavily and visibility became very poor. We had to drive with our lights on and reduce the speed drastically. We got to Kericho around 4:00pm and temporarily pulled over to the roadside to deliberate on whether to continue with the journey or sleepover till the following morning. The consensus was to continue with the journey to save time as we had over a hundred kilometers to cover. Spending the night would have meant wasting valuable time travelling the next day instead of working. We chose work over safety.

Thirty minutes after restarting our journey, we came to a very treacherous part of the road. After a town called Kapsoit, I drove over a series of rubble strips which I didn't think much about. Having gone over the last set of rubble strips, I noticed a sudden sharp bend on the left side of the road. In a flash, there was an oncoming trailer right in the middle of the road. Instinctively I stepped on the brakes and immediately concepts I had learnt in high school physics came into play. Whenever a moving body is going round in a controlled motion, there is an apparent force called a centripetal force pulling it towards the centre of the apparent circle. This keeps the body in control. But if that control is lost, an equal and opposite force called centrifugal force pulls the body away from the centre. With the rain, the road was flooded and once I stepped on the brakes **aquaplaning** took place (no traction between the tires and the road surface). I lost control, centrifugal force took over and the car started skidding right into the trailer. An accident was imminent. My last conscious thought was about Ken and his family, despite the fact that I am a family man, I just said a quick prayer, if my departure hour had come, let Ken be spared because I could not bear the guilt of taking him away from his family. With that, I desperately swung the steering wheel 360 degrees towards his side hoping that the last ditch effort would ensure that Ken's side would be spared. The inevitable happened!

The bang was so loud and the lights went off on me. I found myself in total darkness, I knew it was over. I thought that was it, death is total darkness. My mind must have been racing like a formula one car because there were so many flashes of scenes from my life in the short moments that followed. I could also hear some voices but I could not tell whose they were neither could I see who was talking. Suddenly I saw light again and I saw people trying to force the door of the car open with some crude weapons. The whole scenario was very confusing. I saw Ken and thought to myself, you mean Ken is in heaven with me? How?

The events of the next one hour were only recounted to me by Ken and the good samaritans who helped us get out of the wreckage and took us to hospital.

Ken was by my bedside later that evening in siloam hospital in Kericho. He was pleased when he saw me open my eyes and call him by name. He narrated the whole accident scenario. I was so happy to know that the only injury he sustained was a dislocated left thumb.

I understand as they were taking me to hospital, I engaged them in a discussion and what shocked them is that I asked them whether I was dead.

Upon asking that question Ken told me not to be silly… "How can you be dead and yet you are talking to us?" Ken told me he was even more shocked by the answer I gave…"How sure are you that you are also not dead because I am sure dead people should be able to communicate with each other?" At that juncture they all looked at each other and knew they had to get me to hospital as quickly as they could.

Strange enough even in such difficult moments one can still find humor. Ken told me the decision to take me to a private hospital was made easier by the fact that I was clutching onto a bundle of 1000 shilling notes with a vice like grip on my left hand and they concluded any hospital would accept to admit me on grounds that I had money for deposit which is usually a requirement by private hospitals here in Kenya. The truth is, they tried to get the money from me but the grip was so tight they gave up. To them that was real proof of an old myth of how you cannot separate "A Kikuyu from his money." I happen to come from the Kikuyu community.

To date, I am still amazed by that story because if I remember correctly, I had put the money under the driver's seat as I set out for the journey. It is still a mystery how and when I got it from under the seat. They told me the grip only loosened when the nurse sedated me before taking me to theatre. Ken left the following morning for home to be with his family but I had to be in hospital for a while longer. I had sustained some serious injuries on my legs and I had cracked ribs. I was in so much pain when I woke up the following morning. Anything I did from breathing, speaking, eating to whatever kind of movement caused a lot of pain to my chest cavity. My right leg was heavily bandaged but had no plaster which gave me great relief because I knew it was not broken. When the nurse came to bring me breakfast, I enquired from her my exact state when I was brought to hospital. She confirmed that I was so lucky not to have broken bones. However, she told me my right foot was badly damaged at the ankle joint and my right knee had sustained a long deep cut that had exposed the patella. I had undergone minor surgery to remove glass pieces from the same.

My stay in hospital was made easier and bearable by the fact that my wife and my elder brother, Charles had travelled all the way to Kericho to be with me. I was discharged after a week. I requested to see what remained of the car. The wreckage was at Kericho police station. When I saw it, I knew God had saved me from certain death. The driver's side looked like a piece of cloth that a beast had chewed and then spat out. I could not understand how I had escaped without any head injuries, and no serious injuries above the waist. Even though I was on crutches, I decided to go closer and analyze the wreckage further. I discovered something very unusual in the car, the back rest of the driver's seat was broken and was lying flat towards the back. That began to make sense to me. I reckoned on impact the jerk from the safety belt pulled me so hard that the back thrust, broke the seat and I fell backwards which spared me from what could have been a slaughter by the car's smashed windscreen and bonnet. The bonnet had been split into two. One piece had been pushed right through the windscreen to where my head would have been; had the back rest not given way. Talk about divine intervention! When I later saw the shirt and the tie I was wearing during the accident, I understood perfectly the force on the safety belt. The friction had literally burnt the tie and the shirt.. It is then that I sang "Amazing Grace how sweet the sound, that saved a wretch like me from a wreck like this" The journey home was torturous as my ribs had not completely healed. The road was not all smooth, any bumps, potholes or just uneven road surface caused me extreme discomfort.

Three days after being discharged from hospital I had the most profound of dreams. I dreamt that I was in a beautiful cozy corner office on top floor of a modern skyscraper. I was sitting on a state of the art seat which had fancy buttons on the arm rests. I started playing with the buttons. Upon pressing one of them, the seat went right through the building downwards and I landed in the basement, in front of a huge black gate which had some grill fenestrations. Through the fenestration I saw some scaring red tongs of a big fork-like instrument and then heard an even more scaring deep voice coming from somewhere inside. The voice simply said, "I will be right with you." The voice was so loud it made the building shake. I panicked and I started frantically fumbling with the seat buttons again hoping I could press one that would make the seat fly out of there! I was so sure that was the devil's voice! I pressed one that sent the seat upward right through the roof. It flew and landed into a forest. I was so sure 'he' was running after me, when the seat landed I took off for my dear life!

As I was about to run out of breath, I saw his dirty claws on either side of my body going for my ribs and I knew it was all over for me. But right at that moment, when I was about to give up, a blinding light appeared in front of me and I saw the image of Jesus and he said with the most re-assuring of voices. "Do not worry, he cannot touch you. You belong to me!"

It was at that point that I woke up sweating profusely. I woke my wife up and when she looked at me, she was so worried. The sweat on my face was so much, she asked me whether I was sick, I assured her I was okay, it was just a harrowing dream I had. We both got out of bed and went to the sitting room where I shared my dream with her. I told her I had decided to let the will of God prevail in my life from that moment onwards.

To me, the dream was not just a dream. It was a visitation that got me thinking deeply. I came to the conclusion that God had saved me from the accident for a good reason. I knew my work here on earth was not done. I resolved to do my work to the best of my ability for the glory of God.

The test of my resolve was to happen the very next day. Just after breakfast, I got a call from the insurance company whose work I was going to finish in Kakamega before the accident. The caller was very brief and to the point. He simply said they needed their project completed and since it had stalled because of my accident they had decided to engage somebody else to finish it at my cost. This was not the kind of information that one would just shout 'halleluyah' to. I got numb just thinking how unfair life can be. I quickly reflected on the events of the last two weeks, first the accident, then the bills, then the dream and now close to losing 1.5 million shillings if I did not finish the project. With my young family, I could not afford to lose this project and the earnings from it. After what looked like eternal silence, I told the gentleman on the other end of the line that I was prepared to go to Kakamega despite my condition to finish the job. He did not sound convinced because he knew I was still on crutches and had near zero mobility. I asked myself, "Since I started the project, if anyone had to finish it "Why Not Me?" He finally accepted my pleas but gave me a condition. The job had to be finished within two weeks; failure to which the company would surcharge me for every extra day.

It is when chips are down that you really know who your support pillars are. My wife was my strength. When I told her about my plans, she had no objections even though she was worried about how I would travel. I assured her I would work out a way. I called my friend Ken to make arrangements to go to Kakamega and finish what we started. Ken simply said I was crazy but he did not argue with me.

I knew I could not stand travelling from Thika to Kakamega by road, a distance of over 400km. I organized to take a flight to Kisumu then take a taxi to Kakamega. I camped in Kakamega for two weeks and finished the project. The client was so happy with my work despite the challenges, keep giving me work up to date.

This was a real turn around for me in my life. It was a reminder of Robert Schuller's famous quote, ***"Tough times never last but tough people do."*** After the accident, my professional career really thrived. I have done more architectural work in the last six years since the accident than I had done for

Fourteen years before the accident. However, I still had a deep rooted need to do more but I did not know what more. I thank God that now I know. I know why I had that feeling of emptiness. Putting together this book is hopefully just the beginning of many more.

The man who knows how will always have a job, but the man who knows why will always be his boss."

~RALPH WALDO EMERSON

Ralph Waldo Emerson once said, "The man who knows how will always have a job, but the man who knows why will always be his boss."

Know your 'Why'. Take charge of your life. Be the Boss!

#2

INNOCENT COURAGE

"Courage is rightly esteemed the first of human qualities...
because it is the quality that guarantees all others."

WINSTON CHURCHILL

Do you remember how your life was like when you were a child? Did you see any obstacles to anything you wanted to do? Was it a case of do first and think later if any thinking was needed at all? That was certainly the case with me. In the flashes I had after the accident, I saw myself pleading with my nursery school teacher to let me stay in school.

To move from being just among the others and be the one, it is important to know what you want to achieve. Always start with the end in mind! Then you have to decide how but most critically you must execute your plans of achieving it with single minded determination. It is called focus!

There is a story given in the Bible of David versus Goliath. This story is simply amazing. This is a story of a courageous young man versus a giant. David, an Israelite, the youngest son of a man called Jesse was a small teenage herds' boy. Goliath was a Philistine giant warrior famed for his conquests in battle. Goliath was over nine foot tall, a real giant by any stretch of imagination. The Philistines had declared war on the Israelites. For 40 continuous days, Goliath taunted, mocked and challenged the Israelites to fight. The King of Israel then, Saul and his entire Israel army were terrified. Nobody wanted to face Goliath. Then one day David was sent to the battle lines by his father to go and bring him news of his brothers. While there, he heard Goliath shouting his daily defiance and he saw the great fear stirred within the men of Israel. The young boy could not understand why the Israel men were terrified of Goliath and as he called him, an uncircumcised man. David offered to fight

To move from being just among the others and be the one, it is important to know what you want to achieve.

Goliath. It took quite some persuasion for Saul to agree to it but finally he did. Whenever I think about it, I cannot stop wondering, 'what was David thinking?' I often imagine him, a small boy armed with nothing more than a sling and five small stones, approaching this 9 foot monster who was battle hardened. Goliath had the appropriate battle armor, a CV as a killing machine and David, a herds' boy had the audacity to think he would succeed where seasoned soldiers had failed?

A child sees no obstacles. A child only sees possibilities.

What did David have that enabled him to overcome such an obstacle? I have always opined that David's greatest weapon was his innocent courage and that is what God loved in him and He helped David fight his battles even with the lions that attacked his sheep in the fields. David thought like a child and went ahead to execute his plan just like a child would. A child sees no obstacles. A child only sees possibilities. What a child wants, usually a child gets. This usually happens because a child is innocent, a child is courageous, a child sees the end and not the journey and when you see the end, you will find a way to overcome the hurdles along the journey. Whenever you want to achieve something, it is important to start with the end in mind, then plan your journey, and execute.

Whenever you think like a child your mind is clear, it has no clutter, it is focused. That is a real recipe for success.

I usually imagine what the seasoned soldiers perhaps said of Goliath, *"He is so big he will crash us."* Then I imagine David telling himself, *"He is so big I cannot miss."* Talk about focus! While others saw a mighty crashing giant, David saw a big target that was hard to miss! David analyzed his adversary and saw there was a part of his forehead that was not covered by the helmet. You know, a part of a giant's forehead is still a big part. Armed with his sling and a stone, David aimed at Goliath's forehead and that is what he got. He felled a giant because of thinking like a child and focusing like a child but most importantly, because he was courageous! Whenever you think like a child your mind is clear, it has no clutter, it is focused. That is a real recipe for success.

Robin Sharma says, *'what you focus on grows, what you think about expands, what you dwell upon leads you to your destiny'.*

The story of David reminds me of my personal experience when I was just five years old. I grew up in a typical rural Kenyan village. I was the eighth born in a family of ten. We depended on just an acre of land for food. Those were the days everybody had cash crops and therefore three quarters of our land had coffee, leaving only a small portion for food crops. Needless to say the food from the farm was not enough for the twelve of us and the amount of coffee we had was also not a very viable economic venture to supplement the food and take care of other needs. Our dear mother used to make pots as a way of making up for the needs deficit. There were days she would go to the market to sell the pots and fail to make a sale. She would walk back home in the evening with no coin. Since she did not want to discourage us with the bad news of not having made any sale and therefore having not been able to buy any food, she would put water in a pot and place it on the traditional three stone 'cooker', which used firewood as fuel. Then she would light the fire and start telling us bible stories. She was such a good story teller. She would tell us endless interesting stories until we forgot our hunger and fell asleep. Whenever I think about this I know for sure spiritual food really works. The following morning she would do her motherly magic, get something from the neighbor and we would have something for breakfast.

I always used to envy my school going siblings because at 10:00 o'clock they got porridge in school. That meant they were at least assured of something in their stomach at some point during the day. It was not the case for those at home. I was looking forward to the day I would join school and enjoy the porridge at 10 o'clock. I really pestered my mother to take me to school but she said I was not of school going age yet and that my time would come.

Indeed My time did come.

When I was six years old my mother took me for an interview to join nursery school in the village. Those days we did not have the system practiced nowadays by parents of transferring parenting duties to teachers when the babies are only 3 years. They are made to join baby class, then nursery one and finally pre-unit before joining standard 1. In our time we were allowed to be kids, to play, roll in the mud, herd the goats and cows and do whatever else made you a kid. For most of us at age six it was time to go for the big interview? And it came to pass that my big day was finally with us. The interview was of the craziest kind. It was not aimed at knowing what you knew or did not know. It was not a question and answer kind of interview. The teacher simply told you to put your right hand right over your head and try and touch your left ear. I know you will try and do it as you read this. Right now at your age, that is easy but when you were in your early years of existence nothing could have been harder.

As fate would have it, I could not touch my left ear with my right hand over my head so I failed the interview. That devastated me. Being the eighth born in our family, I had watched my elder brothers and sisters wear school uniform, win awards whey they had performed well in school and it looked really cool. I couldn't wait to join school. I always used to ask my mum "Why Not Me.? She would always tell me to wait for my turn.

Now here I was, six years old, with an opportunity to start school but I had failed the 'interview'. The teacher noticed the sadness on my face, placed her hand on my shoulder and with a lot of motherliness told me not to worry because I would have another chance the following year. That was not good enough for me, so I quickly thought of a solution and I asked her; "can I try placing my left hand over my head and touch my right ear?" She looked at me and said, "If your right hand cannot touch your left ear, then your left hand cannot touch your right ear, but you can try." I did and I failed. I was not prepared to stay at home for another year. I asked her another question;

"Can you please allow me to stay in school for one week and see whether by the end of the week I will have learnt how to touch my ear?" She looked at me with consternation and said; "You cannot learn how to do that, you have to grow a little bigger." I guess the teacher never saw what was coming next. I told her all the others who had passed the interview were the same age as me and I could learn how to touch my ear just like them ……or so I thought.

The teacher happened to by my aunt and she had had enough of my 'nuisance' so she just gave in and gave me the chance with a stern warning that if it did not happen within a week, I would be back home. Getting that chance was the happiest time of my life. I promised myself that I would practice every day until I touched my ear. Every morning I would dutifully go in front of the teacher and draw her attention as I tried it. It never worked. By the end of the week I could tell I had become the teacher's favorite by the way she treated me. I was sad because I knew I had not passed the interview yet. I knew I would be sent home. I went to school on Friday morning expecting the worst but still hoping my hand had grown longer and the miracle would happen. As was my routine for the week, I went straight to the teacher's desk and tried one more desperate time to no avail. All the other kids were laughing at me.

persistence and determination had won me the admission.

The teacher looked at me and smiled, I did not know what to make of the smile. She finally extended her hand to me and as I shook it with tears in my eyes expecting a goodbye, she said to the class; "Let us officially welcome Stephen to the class." She told the class that my persistence and determination had won me the admission.

Persistence certainly wears out resistance. Robert Kiyosaki says; ***"Failure defeats losers; failure inspires winners"*** I won because I had the winning mentality of a child. I chose to see the possibilities not the obstacles. I had the courage to push for what I wanted.

How many times do we miss out on opportunities because we chose to see the obstacles instead?

How many times do we miss out on opportunities because we chose to see the obstacles instead? Always remember this, Paulo Coelho, The Alchemist said, "***If you want something so badly, the whole universe conspires to let you have it.***"

#3

THE POWER OF A POSITIVE MIND

Have you ever been approached by a street urchin for help? What was your response? Do you know a positive response could be the spark needed to change such a child's life?

In one of the flashes after my accident, I saw Simon driving a beautiful car into a big factory. Simon is a boy I met in Thika just after I started my own practice way back in 1994. One day as I was going to board a matatu (Public Service Vehicle) to go home, a street boy stopped me and asked me to buy him a cup of tea. He said he was feeling very cold and had not eaten anything all day. He was different from all the street kids I had encountered before. Every other street kid I had met before would demand for money and would really pester you. Whether you gave them or not they would quickly run off to the next target and some would say something nasty to you if you did not give them anything. But this boy was different. He did not want me to give him money for tea, he wanted me to go into a restaurant and buy him the tea. I thought that was just cool. Luckily we were just outside a restaurant. We went in for tea. I told him he could have a meal as well. I expected him to get excited and say; Yes! Yes! Yes! Simon looked at me and said, "I don't want to bother you too much, it is good enough that you have agreed to sit with me, a lot of people just walk away without noticing me, a cup of tea will be just fine." That coming from a street boy who I was sure had not eaten any square meal that day broke me down. I had to restrain myself from shedding tears in his presence. I excused myself to go to the restrooms and instructed a waiter to serve him with some French fries and a sausage. I found him staring at the food not sure whether to touch it or not because as he told me, he was afraid it may not have been meant for him. Once I assured him it was his; he ate and I could see he was really grateful.

"You do not ask for too much information from a hungry man, first feed him."

I really wanted to know this boy's background but I let him finish his food before asking him too many questions. There is a saying where I come from that, "You do not ask for too much information from a hungry man, first feed him." Once he was done eating, he gave me his story. He had recently lost his parents and the relatives were mistreating him so much that he opted to look for refuge in the streets. That is the typical story you would generally hear from street children, sometimes genuine and sometimes not. But his sounded genuine. I decided to give Simon some advice that would hopefully help him to eventually stop begging and start earning. I told him to start going to offices in the morning to ask them whether he could be of assistance to them by way of emptying their waste paper baskets or just running errands for them in town. I told him to start with my office. In my community we say, "A hardworking child can never lack somebody to wash his feet."

"A hardworking child can never lack somebody to wash his feet."

The next morning just as I was settling at my desk Simon came and he looked so enthusiastic to report to 'duty'. Just seeing him there asking me whether he could be of assistance made me realize that Simon had a key ingredient required for success in life; a positive attitude. I decided I would do everything I could to assist him get off the streets completely. I gave him work to dust my small office and referred him to a few other offices where he would do the same and earn some money. I had a bigger agenda for him. Once he had done this routine for two weeks, I sat him down in my office and asked him whether he would want to go to school. It was as if he was waiting for that question. He was very excited, he said yes! He told me he had dropped out at class five and that if he got a chance to go back, he would really appreciate.

I talked to a friend of mine and together we organized how to get Simon back to school. He went through primary school, secondary school and eventually college. He studied some basic computer packages in college. When he finished he finished, he requested me to assist him look for a job. Looking for a job in this country is never easy. After several months of trying to get a job without success, I decided to sell him an idea. I asked him whether he was interested in business. I casually shared with him the story of Africa's richest man, Aliko Dangote and how he started small and grew his business to the multi billion Empire it is today.

Even though Simon did not have any idea who Dangote was, he was very positive about the idea, the challenge was what kind of business and the seed capital. Luckily he got a temporary job in an office and I advised him to take it as he developed the business idea in his mind.

I moved my office to another part of town and I lost touch with Simon for quite a while. Early 2015 I bumped into him in one of the streets of Thika. He looked so different. His face was so radiant. He was elegantly dressed. I had to take a step back and look again to be sure it was Simon. It was him alright. Wow! What a transformation! We exchanged niceties and we stood on the side of the street updating each other on what has been going on in our lives since we last met. I was so happy to hear his update. After doing the temporary job for six months he had saved some money and decided to resign to start a business.

I was so curious to know what business he had started. He had noticed that working class people were always in a hurry and had little time to do shopping for fruits and vegetables in the market. These commodities were so expensive in the supermarkets, he had decided to set up a fruit 'parlor' on the street where we first met to sell fruits cheaply to people as they went to board public service vehicles for home. I thought it was a brilliant idea. I promised to visit him some day. A week later I visited Simon. It was a hot sunny day. I had planned to pick him up for some fresh juice in a restaurant nearby as we chatted. When I got to his fruit 'parlor' I was pleasantly surprised to find him selling fresh fruit and blending fresh juice for his customers. He was very busy serving customers. I ordered some juice as I waited for him to finish with other customers. Looking at him serving customers made me feel so proud of him. He had clearly not just started a business; he had learnt and was applying the rules of business. He was talking to them and serving them cheerfully. Because of the conversations he had with his customers some took more to support this young entrepreneur's budding business. Simon clearly had a knack for identifying business opportunities!

We later got a chance to talk and what he shared amazed me. First he had secured all the necessary permits from the Local Authority to operate, his business was legal. The best part of his business story was the numbers. He said that on average he sells 200 glasses of juice per day at the cost of fifty shillings each which makes his total juice sales an average of Ten thousand shillings daily. His average fruits sale per day was four thousand shillings. If you do your math, his total sales are fourteen thousand shillings daily. Even if his profit margin was to be a modest 50% of his sales, He clearly makes a profit of seven thousand shillings a day which would translate to two hundred and ten thousand shillings a month. If I may ask how many employed Kenyans earn that kind of money as salary? Your guess is as good as mine.

Simon's shop is a hand cart placed strategically on the road side where there is maximum pedestrian flow. He has a big dream, he wants to have a beautiful fruit parlor and a juice factory and employ many people. He wants to be the next Dangote. I told him, you know what buddy, *"Your dreams are valid."* By the look of it, it will not be long before he realizes his dream.

Simon's story just inspires me and I am so glad to have met him when I did. He says that agreeing to get into a restaurant and sit with him for a cup of tea made him regain faith in humanity again and it gave him impetus to believe in the good that still exists in people including himself. I always tell him it is mainly his positive attitude and his determination that has propelled him to where he is and will continue to propel him even further. Believe it or not Simon told me that those from his parents' family who had thrown him out now seek him out and will not make any family decisions without consulting him. He has become the corner stone that the builders had rejected. Simon agreed to change his thinking. By changing his thinking, he changed his life. He did not go looking for opportunities in some far away land; he identified them right where we had first met, in the street. This reminded me of Russel Conwell's famous speech, 'Acres of Diamond.' If I may ask you, where are you looking for your treasure? Your treasure could be right where you are; on the streets, in a kitchen, in a farm, in dump site, wherever you may be. The most important lesson to learn here is that wherever your external treasure may be, what will help you get it is the treasure from within you, your positive attitude!

If I may ask you, where are you looking for your treasure? Your treasure could be right where you are

The story of Simon's attitude resonates in a way to something that happened to me in 1975 when I was in standard one. One day as I was going home in the evening, I experienced sharp piecing pains on my lower abdomen and on my thighs. My thighs felt like they were being poked with sharp objects. Our home was about 4 kilometers from school and I had just gone half way. I decided to ignore the pain at first but the intensity increased to unbearable levels. My legs could hardly support my body. Eventually I collapsed and passed out. When I came to, I was in a hospital somewhere in Thika town. I remember seeing my mother and my elder brother by my hospital

The most important lesson to learn here is that wherever your external treasure may be, what will help you get it is the treasure from within you, your positive attitude!

bedside. I was to later learn from my mother that some good Samaritans had picked me up from the road side and taken me home from where my mother organized to take me to hospital in Thika where my elder brother was working. In the few moments that ensued after coming to, I overheard the doctor telling my mother that his prognosis of my situation was not good. According to him, I did not have much longer to live. He said my kidneys were failing and he could not see a way out. My mother being the staunch Christian she is could not stomach that! How could the doctor play God with her son's life? She got so furious and she reprimanded the doctor. She said he was not to touch me again and that she was taking me away from there immediately. The next thing I knew we were in a public service vehicle on our way to Murang'a district general hospital. I tell you mothers are special! While undergoing treatment in Murang'a hospital, a nurse developed a special liking for me and used to talk to me even beyond official hours. I remember her telling me that I had to be strong and very positive in order to get well. She said I had to do it for my mother. One day she asked me, "Do you remember the boy who was on the next bed?" I said, yes, what about him? She said the boy had a similar condition and had felt better and discharged. She said, "If he could get well, ask yourself, "why not me?" That gave me renewed hope and a resolve to fight off my illness. My mother and the nurse had a positive attitude which rubbed me on. I believe it was what gave me the courage to fight the disease every day. I was in hospital for two months, I eventually got better, was discharged and resumed school. If it was not for my mother's faith and positive attitude, if it was not for the nurse's positive attitude and encouragement, if it was not for my accepting to embrace a positive attitude, who knows what could have happened. But here I am forty years later sharing the story with you. And I lived to meet and help Simon get off the street.

How many Simons are out there? As you read this, you could be the Simon or the Simon discoverer. Whatever your position, your positive attitude will determine whether Simon remains on the street or goes on to fulfill his dream of becoming the next Dangote. Your positive attitude will determine whether you overcome or succumb to your circumstances.

Your positive attitude will determine whether you overcome or succumb to your circumstances.

Always remember this; ***"Your Attitude, not your Aptitude will determine your Altitude in life."***

#4

IDENTIFYING AND OBEYING THE STOP SIGNS

How many times have you been in a situation where you want to do something but a small inner voice tells you not to or vice versa? How many times have you ignored that voice? What were the consequences? Do you feel like you wish you obeyed the small inner voice?

The journey of life is like driving or walking in the city. It has traffic lights. The red light says "stop" the amber light says 'get ready' and the green light tells you 'go'. The red light is the hazard light, it is the danger light. If you jump the red light, chances are you will either cause an accident or be arrested for careless driving and fined for it. There are many times in life when we ignore the red light to our detriment. If you want to get to your life's journey destination safely, learn to identify the red light. What is the red light in your life's journey? If you reflect on your life you will realize there are times when you think you have put your best foot forward, you have invested heavily in a venture but the results are disastrous. Remember the times you got a job with a good salary, a beautiful office with all the trappings that come with a plush job but you still felt empty. Remember the times you dated someone who looked gorgeous, you were the envy of all your peers but there was something about the person that did not feel right to you? Remember the times you got into a vehicle, but you did not feel right about it? Remember the time you registered for a course and after starting, you felt you

The red light is the hazard light, it is the danger light.

There are many times in life when we ignore the red light to our detriment. If you want to get to your life's journey destination safely, learn to identify the red light.

needed to change it?

These are all stop signs in life. They are the red light. When that happens, it is time to stop and take stock of your life. It is time to have very serious conversations with self and chart a new route. If you do not, you risk encountering a serious life accident ahead.

Everyone has an inner voice that either consents or rejects your plans or methods of execution.

The stop signs can be identified by simply listening to your inner voice, your inner self. Everyone has an inner voice that either consents or rejects your plans or methods of execution. The inner voice is always right. The inner voice is God in you. Learn to obey it.

I reflect on my accident and I see that I failed to see the stop signs. I refused to obey them. The tire puncture was the first sign. The heavy rains were the second sign. The inner voice even told me to pull over and look for accommodation in Kericho but I over ruled it with near fatal consequences.

I have a very good friend called John. He was initially trained as a diploma teacher. I first met him during a long vacation from my university studies at a school where I was engaged as a Mathematics teacher for the duration of the vacation. He was also teaching there and he was quite the teacher. When I met him again, he had abandoned teaching and was working at a hardware shop. Thereafter he quit working and started doing business. He has very good PR and therefore it was very easy for him to seal business deals. Within a year of starting his business, he bought a car. Things were looking bright for John but he always said his money did not last. He said that as soon as he got paid, the money would somehow disappear. "Does this sound familiar? I thought so." John was always very busy looking for new business which he would get, do it with consummate ease, get paid, use up the money and the vicious cycle would continue. There seemed to be no certainty in his life.

The only certain thing was he would get good business, get paid, use up the money and quickly get broke again. The tragedy was that the money was never invested. At some point the business well dried up and life became really hard for him. At the age of 44 years, he had no wife and no children. In our African culture at that age society expects you to be a settled family man with big children. The societal pressure was also beginning to tell on him.

It got to a point where John did not even have an office of his own to operate from. I accommodated him in my office. He is really a fun guy to have around and very intelligent too. I was happy to have helped him out. One day he decided to start an NGO to fight tribalism in our country and he Inco-operated me and a mutual friend as directors. He came up with a brilliant name for it (SIDIK- an acronym for Strength In Diversity Kenya). We developed a beautiful strategy. We visited high offices to see whether we could get funding but all our efforts came a cropper. I even sponsored a trophy during a National secondary Schools drama festival on behalf of SIDIK hoping this would give the NGO some mileage. I thought perhaps this would help the NGO start its activities and make John stable. It did not work as planned.

One day he said he had decided to go back to teaching. He had applied to the Teachers service commission and had been posted to a primary school in his rural area in western Kenya. At first I thought John was going backwards in his life, how could he agree to go and teach in a primary school? It just did not make sense to me. But I did not want to discourage him. I wished him well.

A year later I got some contract near the school where he was teaching and during my first site visit, I decided to call on him. What I found was beyond my wildest imagination. John had married and they were expecting a baby. He had also enrolled for a school based degree program at Kenyatta university tailor made for teachers to study during school holidays. He

'The most powerful weapon on earth is the human soul on fire with purpose and passion'.

-FERDINAND FOCH

looked transformed. He was a soul on fire. Looking at him reminded me of what Ferdinand Foch once said; 'The most powerful weapon on earth is the human soul on fire with purpose and passion'. He was on a mission. He graduated after three years and emerged top of his class with first class honors. Due to his outstanding performance, he got a scholarship to do a masters' degree in Dar es salaam University in Tanzania. As I write this, he has since finished his masters' degree and contemplating doing his PHD. He enrolled his wife for a course and got her a good job at the public service. They have been blessed with the second child and as things seem, John has never been happier.

All those failed businesses, the stalled NGO project were STOP signs in John's life. He needed this to reconnect with his destiny. His destiny was teaching, his destiny was in pursuit of further studies. His destiny was in getting married and bringing up a family. It may have happened at a more advanced age than for the average African man but it is never too late to reconnect with your destiny. After all, nobody knows how long he is going to live. For all I know John could be here to see his great grandchildren.

"The two most important days in a man's life are the day he was born and the day he discovers why he was born."

-MARK TWAIN

The key thing is he identified the stop signs, he obeyed them. He listened to his inner self and obeyed it. He made a conscious decision to reconnect with his destiny.

Mark twain said, "The two most important days in a man's life are the day he was born and the day he discovers why he was born."

When you discover your destiny, you live a very fulfilling life. A story is told that one day Winston Churchill was going to give a live interview in BBC studios. The interview was to start at 6:00pm. He decided to take a cab to the studio. The cab driver warned him that if the traffic became so bad he would drop him off because he wanted to go back and be in his house by 6:00pm. As they went along, the traffic started building up and just about a hundred meters to the studio there was a grid lock. The driver asked him to kindly disembark as earlier agreed because he had to go back. Churchill asked him what was so important that he had to get back home at 6:00pm. The driver asked him "where do you live"? Haven't you heard that Winston Churchill will be interviewed live on BBC at 6:00pm? At that moment, Churchill decided to identify himself and I can only imagine the shock on the driver's face. He was hurriedly trying to drop Churchill off so as to go back home and watch Churchill live on T.V. How many of us are running away from our destiny because we have not identified it?

Stop signs exist to redirect us to our destinies. If you listen to your inner voice, your intuition, you will see the stop signs.

Stop signs exist to redirect us to our destinies.

Here are some of the tips to help you start tapping into your intuition:

#1. Listen

Start listening to yourself and to the signs the universe is displaying all around you.

#2. Live in the present moment

The past is in the past. The future has not come yet. Just focus on now, how are you feeling right now. Once you are able to live more in the present moment without worrying about the future and the past, you will be able to listen more closely.

#3. Be Mindful
Stop rushing through life. Everything you do should be done mindfully. This goes along with being present. You cannot do something mindfully if you are not present

#4. Meditate
This is scary for some people. Just sit for a few minutes each day with yourself with no distractions. Start to see what comes up in your mind, try to quiet your mind and then see what comes up again. Meditation is a great way to really get to know your true self.

#5. Be Confident
Start to embrace who you truly are. Your true inner self and be confident in that person. That person is beautiful, smart and powerful. Believe it!

You need these five steps in order to see the stop signs and follow your destiny.

#5

WILL POWER

How many times have you given up on something because you think you will never make it only to realize you were so close and all you needed was to be more resilient? Do you know people who are more successful than you are not smarter than you? Successful people just happen to have more resilience, more patience, higher endurance and they simply just have a very strong will power. They never give up. No wonder it is said, 'where there is a will, there is a way.'

I met this wonderful lady called Nana Wanjau, the President of Rotary Club of Nairobi East and she shared with me a story that was such a profound testament of what will power can do and what the lack of it can mean.

'where there is a will, there is a way.'

The Rotary club planned to take members for a mountain climbing exercise. They were to scale the heights of Mt. Kilimanjaro, the second highest mountain in the world. This was the first time Nana was going to climb Mt. Kilimanjaro. In preparation for the exercise they did a lot of practice including climbing mount Longonot, Ngong hills and Kilimambogo. Nana had to make very tough personal decisions because the date that was agreed upon for the journey from Nairobi to the foot of the mountain was just a day after she was to get back from a family holiday abroad. As a committed family person, she was in a dilemma but after wise counsel from a mentor, she opted not to interfere with the family holiday as it had already been pre-arranged. She instead opted to push her body and have no break between flying in from the holiday and the mountain climbing. This decision was made easier for her by the fact that she had managed to convince her husband who is not a member of the rotary club to join her for the mountain climbing.

At the time of the mountain climbing exercise, Nana was not the President, she was the president-elect. She had made up her mind that she would use this exercise and the experiences there off to assess some key qualities of members of the club. She knew it would reveal a lot about the members including her. She never shared this with anyone. I found this very interesting and I was curious to know why. Nana is not one to summarize a story and she kept me guessing. In her narration, she mentioned that she had turned down to serve as President twice before for family reasons. It was not the right time for her, her children were too young. She had finally accepted on the third and her plan was to have everything in perfect order or at least close to it. Not only did she want the timing to be right, but she also wanted to surround herself with the right people to manage the affairs of the club for her term. Talk about being conscious of the law of the inner circle.

I love the way Nana acknowledges that the past club Presidents had prepared the ground for her smooth take over. She says if she has been able to see far, it is because she stands on the shoulders of such giants as the past leadership.

Nana, her husband and a team of 37 people set off from Nairobi to the foot of Kilimanjaro hours after arriving from the family holiday. She reckons she was physically fit as she is a stickler to regular exercise and she was also mentally set for it. Being the president-elect, this was an excellent opportunity for her to demonstrate service leadership. Nana made a decision after their arrival at the foot of the mountain that she would stick with the weakest link in the group to support them. The first day, she reckons, was just a walk in the park. There was nothing challenging. All she was interested in was to connect, bond and encourage the team.

On the second day, she was the last to leave the camp just to make sure nobody was left behind. She was practicing every law of leadership. As they progressed up the mountain, the effect of high altitude started to be felt. You could almost feel the cloud thickness, she said. The clouds were so low one could almost literally touch them. Everyone was very excited. The enthusiasm was palpable. When they got to the camp, the mood, the stories could not have been better. Everyone was looking forward to the next day.

Morning came and the third day was here. A lady in the team got seriously sick. She had nausea and a running stomach. Nana decided she had to be with her. As everyone else left the camp, Nana and the guard were left attending to the sick lady. By the time everything settled, the rest of the team was already way ahead. Nana and the lady were the last. In her estimation they were behind the first team by two hours. They were really struggling to get to the next stop-over point which was also to be the lunch point. Communication between them and the rest of the team was made impossible by the fact that the guard who was supposed to have a communication radio, for some inexplicable reasons did not have it. The condition of the lady was getting worse. They soldiered on despite the fact that they were very tired, very hungry and exhausted. It is usually said that sometimes everything that could possibly go wrong does. Nana was to experience this first hand.

In a flash, the weather changed for the worse. It had been warm but all of a sudden without warning the heavens opened and down came hailstorms. Nana was dressed in a sleeveless vest. The hailstorms were hitting her exposed skin so hard that they bruised her. With the sick lady, the worst weather and with no communication radio things were looking hopeless for them. They kept pushing themselves to get to the lunch point. This would ensure that at least they could catch up with the rest of the group and get some food and assistance. Luckily for them the hailstorm stopped and eventually they got to the lunch point. The worst was awaiting Nana, she had given her lunch box to her husband to carry for her but he and the entire first group were nowhere in sight. Nana could not comprehend what was happening to her, things could not possibly get worse. After all the struggles with the

'You do not know how strong you are until being strong is the only option you have'

-BOB MARLEY

sick lady her husband could afford to leave with her lunch box? This was too much for her to bear. "How could he?" She was going through a roller coaster of emotions. Her heart was so heavy it was hurting. She knew this was going to be a defining moment for her, her relationship with her husband and the remainder of the trip. She decided to walk away from the rest of her group members to allow them to have their lunch. She needed to have a deep conversation with herself and she did.

It is Bob Marley who said, 'You do not know how strong you are until being strong is the only option you have'

"Only carry the luggage not the baggage."

Nana decided to be strong. She had no choice. Bitterness was not an option. Giving up was not an option either. She decided her only options were to forgive her husband and push herself to the next camp with her team. Out of that experience she even coined a phrase which has become her mantra in life; "Only carry the luggage not the baggage."

They started off again, Nana was feeling much lighter in her heart and she was actually looking forward to meeting him. When they got to camp she was literally looking for him to hug him. Her decision to forgive had given her renewed energy to move on and conquer the mountain. Her will power was at work!

Do you know life's journey is like that? Success sometimes is hindered by our refusal to let go of our baggage. We let our pasts dictate our future. We let our failures define us. If you want to move on in life you must embrace the present. It is the only one you have control over. '*The past is a cancelled cheque, the future is a promissory note but the present is your cash at hand. What you do with your present determines the outcome of your future.*'

The fourth and final leg of the climb was to start at night. Everyone had light supper which was simply soup and some bread. They were to have just a few hours of sleep before wake up at 10pm in preparation to start the first phase of the last leg. At 11 pm they set off. Only the sick were left behind. Nana described the night as pitch dark. Everyone had to have a small flashlight attached on their forehead but even that was only enough to show you a silhouette of the person ahead of you. People had to walk in a single file. You could not afford to get off the trail of the one ahead of you otherwise you would get lost in the darkness. Nana says the darkness was so much you could literally feel it. It was the most scaring thing she had ever experienced. The night was also so silent, it was eerie. The only consolation for her was the occasional voice of her husband telling her to step carefully, one step at a time. As they progressed, effects of the darkness, the high altitude, the extreme cold started affecting some of the members. One of the ladies even became delusional, she was shouting saying she did not come to the mountain to die. Some other members started hallucinating saying they were seeing dragons. It was really scary. Nana could only pray for a sign of hope from above.

After what seemed like eternal torture, the sign of hope everyone was waiting for came. The pitch darkness suddenly gave way to some beautiful, magical orange glow. The wonderful Kilimanjaro sunrise hit them. Nana says you could hear the sigh of relief from everyone. In her words, it was as if they had just come from, '*the belly of hell to heaven.*'

Eventually they got to the stop-over point which was Gilman's peak, the second highest peak of Mt. Kilimanjaro. From Gilman's peak one could clearly see the highest peak, Uhuru. At Gilman's peak quite a number of people had decided they were not going any further despite the fact that they could clearly see Uhuru peak.

Only twelve members out of the thirty nine made it to the highest peak. Out of the twelve only five were from rotary club of Nairobi East where Nana was the president-elect. She was among the five. She was later to disclose to the members that she was looking for board members to help her run the club during her term of office and everyone from the club who made it to the top automatically had qualified to be in the board. Interestingly, Nana says two characters stood out in that adventure. There was a gentleman who looked every bit like the kind who would definitely make it but he did not, not because he got sick but because he gave up. When he later learnt of Nana's 'hidden agenda' he was very disappointed with himself, he is really looking forward to the next climb so that he can prove to himself that he can do it. Then there is this lady who did not look like she had the physical endurance to conquer the mountain but she did. Nana says that she joined the board and has continued to prove exactly how resilient she is even in how she handles her work and life.

Willpower is character in action.'

My question to you is; 'how many times have you given up on something you had started simply because it appeared like a lost course only to realize later you were just so near the end? If only you had exercised a little more patience, a little more resilience, a little more will power?

I want to conclude this chapter by saying: ***'Willpower is character in action.'*** Your character will ultimately tell by the way you exercise your will power. Remember you are in charge of your willpower. In the words of Nike, go out there and '*just do it*'.

Dan Millman said, "Willpower is the key to success, successful people strive no matter what they feel by applying their will to overcome apathy, doubt or fear."

Let willpower be a big part of your answer to "Why Not Me?"

"Willpower is the key to success, successful people strive no matter what they feel by applying their will to overcome apathy, doubt or fear."

-DAN MILLMAN

#6

IDENTIFYING YOUR STRENGTHS AND PLAYING TO THEM

Do you know your areas of strength? Are you doing trial and error with your life? Are you stuck in a career that does not make you happy? Do you sometimes feel like you are cursed because you have been trying so hard but nothing seems to work? Do you feel like no matter what you do, you are just mark-timing?

A lot of people are doing things that don't give them satisfaction simply because they are not exploiting their full potential. Your full potential can only be realized if you playing to your strengths.

Before you start excelling in life, it is important to first know your life's aim and then manifest your vision in consistent action.

'The distance between you and your vision is simply action!'

Whenever I think of life's aim and vision, I remember my immediate elder brother Venerable Canon Perminus Muiru. He is an archdeacon in the Anglican Church of Kenya. Canon is actually a title of honor bestowed by the Bishop on few selected members of clergy or laity who the Bishop deems fit to be in his inner circle as advisers and helpers. He is an amazing human being. He is a man of the cloth and in his own right very distinguished and respected in the Anglican church of Kenya. He holds a Masters' degree in Christian Ministries. He was never your definition of the sharp kid in school. He was to say the least average. But he had a very solid character from a very early age. I remember he gave his life to Christ in 1977 when he was in standard six and he has never looked back. Many kids of his age and even older did not know what that meant leave alone understanding it. A lot of them would even laugh at him and even mock him. He was barely thirteen. His salvation really pleased my mother. Being a staunch Christian herself, she always prayed for her children to be born again. She was the chairlady of mothers union in our church and our Sunday school teacher. seeing one of her children accept Christ at such an early age was music to her ears. Perminus has had a peculiar pattern in his life right from his birth. He was born on Christmas day the same day we celebrate the birth of Christ in our Christian faith. Indeed it took quite some debate between my mum and dad not to call him Emmanuel which when translated means God with us.

After finishing primary school, he was admitted to a secondary school where he proceeded to become the chairman of the school's Christian union. When he finished form four, he did not make it for advanced level in high school. My elder brother got him a job with B.A.T but he turned it down saying his faith could not allow him to work with a cigarette manufacturer. That was very interesting especially because our parents could have done with financial help from his earnings. But he had his mind made up. He started keeping himself busy making ties out of dried banana barks and preaching to people. Eventually due to his faith and commitment to church work, he got an engagement as a catechist with an Anglican church in Thika. He worked with so much devotion that he became very popular in church. When an opportunity for basic training in theology arose, he was an obvious choice for it and the church sent him to study theology at Bishop Kariuki Theological College. Here he finished among the top students and he was ordained as a clergy.

He had seamlessly fitted into the world of mainstream theology where he always wanted to be. A few years later he applied for a degree course (bachelors of divinity) at St Paul's university, Limuru and graduated with honors. His star continued to shine. He was promoted to higher positions of service in the diocese. Finally he applied for a masters' degree course in Daystar University, completed his studies and graduated without a hitch. Despite the fact that he was not considered very bright in regular school studies, when he enrolled into theological school he excelled. Indeed he was the first one to get a bachelor's and a master's degree in our family. All this was possible because he identified his areas of strength very early. He pursued it relentlessly and he triumphed. If you meet him, he is a very contented person and he is always true to himself. He has grown exponentially in many spheres of life: he is a renowned clergy, a model family man, a much sought after mentor and an ardent farmer. He is a perfect example of a people person. This has also helped to open many investment doors for him. Whereas nobody was clapping for him in primary school, everyone was in theological school. His pattern of life continues to fall in place simply because he plays to his strengths. He is truly inspirational!

'Identify your area of strength and play to it.'

I challenge everyone reading this to do as Perminus did; 'Identify your area of strength and play to it.'

The earlier you do this, the less energy you will waste on irrelevant endeavors. The good news is, it is never too late. If you have been stuck in the wrong career, stuck with the wrong people, you can make the choice today to get your life back on track.

Someone once said that madness is doing the same thing over and over again and expecting different results. Change and get back on track!

madness is doing the same thing over and over again and expecting different results.

Perminus' story is very unique to me because I can give a personal testimony about it but there are numerous stories out there that I can write about. The most outstanding story I would want to share briefly is the one of Bill Gates. This great man whose innovations affect everyone in one way or another in the entire world owes his enormous success and wealth to identifying his strength early on in life and playing to it.

> *"Above all be true to thyself."*
>
> -WILLIAM SHAKESPEAR

Bill gates had benefited from exposure to computers in his early childhood and he had developed a very keen interest in them and because of his interest he had learnt a lot about them.

When he joined university to study computer technology, Bill gates realized that whatever was taught was stuff he already knew. He was way ahead of everyone else because he had taken personal interest early on and studied all he could about computers. He indeed dropped out of college so that he could continue with his quest for more advanced knowledge of the computer world. Bill gates eventually founded Microsoft and he has continued to rule the computer world with his software designs. He has been listed on several occasions as the world's richest man by Forbes magazine.

All this has been possible for him because he identified his area of strength, pursued it relentlessly and has remained true to himself.

William shakespear said; "Above all be true to thyself."

I am a great football fan. Indeed a great fan of Manchester United. Over the years I have noted that the best performances by the team happen when the best players are playing in their natural positions. This is why all coaches have their preferred first team. The best demonstration of this for Manchester united happened during the UEFA Champions league finals in 1999 when they were playing Bayern Munich in Nou camp, Barcelona. Bayern Munich took the lead in the first half through Mathias Sammer and the score remained 1-0 until injury time. Throughout that football season Manchester united had used two striking players as subs and dubbed them super subs to good effect. With the game headed to the end and imminent defeat for Manchester united looming, the coach, Sir Alex Ferguson, sent on his super subs, Teddy Sheringham and Ole Gunnar Solskjeer. Deep into injury time these two strikers lived up to their billing and scored a goal each and helped their team win the UEFA Champions league. These are two players who clearly thrived in being used as super subs. They did not mind not being used for the entire duration of ninety minutes of the game. They knew their strength was coming in as impact players. In that game ninety seconds of injury time is all they required to win the championship for their team. That was a perfect demonstration of playing to people's strengths. Before that game, these two guys were only celebrated in English football. But after their exploits in that game, their names were on the lips of every football fan and sports writer world wide.

When you identify your strengths and play to them, you will graduate from being tolerated to being celebrated.

When you identify your strengths and play to them, you will graduate from being tolerated to being celebrated. You will not have to look for work, work will look for you.

Marilyn Vos Savant said; *'Success is achieved by developing our strengths, not by eliminating our weaknesses.*

Identify and develop your Strengths NOW!

#7

BE YOUR OWN BIGGEST CRITIC

Are you the type of person that fears criticism? Do you go on the defensive every time someone criticizes something you have done? Do you look at critics as unfair, insensitive people?

For a person who wants to learn, for one to improve oneself, one must be willing to embrace criticism. Indeed you must become your own biggest critic. Allow others to subject you and what you do to serious criticism. Allow yourself to look at yourself and what you do through the prism of others' eyes.

"To master others is intelligence, but to master self is real power."

To be able to embrace criticism from others and learn from it, takes courage and wisdom. To be able to criticize yourself is to master self. Someone said; "To master others is intelligence, but to master self is real power."

I have been privileged to work with Mangu High School for the last eleven years and one of the most inspiring things I have learnt from the school is their motto. Their motto is written in Kiswahili, 'Jishinde ushinde'. This translated into English, simply means; '*Conquer yourself in order to conquer others*' or put in another way; '*In order to master others, first master yourself.*' To master yourself, become your own biggest critic. This has over the years formed a fundamental part of the training Mangu High School gives to its students and it is no wonder that the school has gone on to produce some of the most remarkable personalities in our country, including but not limited to former President of Kenya, Mwai Kibaki. The gentleman took up the reigns of leadership in our country while on a wheel chair, he did not have the smoothest of rides during his first term due to his poor health.

His true character came to the fore during his second term, the beginning of which was characterized by post election violence after the disputed 2007 presidential elections, after which it took the intervention of the panel of eminent African persons led by former U.N chief Koffi Anan to calm things down and help form a government of National unity dubbed the Grand coalition.

This was basically a shared government between the president and his political adversary Raila Odinga who became the country's Prime minister. The sharing was deemed necessary so as to appease both sides of the political divide. However, this brought about a lot of suspicions in government and at times open public criticism of what the President was doing from the Prime minister. Politics is politics and someone once described it as a very dirty game. The Grand coalition government was a perfect example of how dirty politics can get. But what I learnt from all the shenanigans was that a person who has learnt to master self can rise above negative criticism, learn from positive criticism and excel. That is what Kibaki did. He was able to steer the country from the post election violence and a failing economy to a commendable level of economic growth and also brought back peace and tranquility in our country.

The best demonstration of being ones best critic has to be the story of Michael Jordan. Michael, the legendary Chicago Bulls basketball player set many records and achieved so many milestones. He is regularly referred to as the greatest basket ball player of all time. What many people do not know is that Michael did not start his career as a great player. He had to evolve. Evolution is the survival of the fittest where the weak ones die out leaving only the strong. Michael Jordan took that same approach with himself. Anytime he found a weakness in himself he worked on it until it became strength. His life is composed of a series of obstacles each of which he turned into an evolutionary step. With each step he discarded another weakness and picked up another strength becoming the Michael Jordan we all know. His life is a story of challenge, of struggle and of ultimate triumph. We should learn all we can from this incredible story. Michael had a lot of critics but he realized that the only way to silence your critics is to work on the area of your weakness until it became strength. Be your biggest critic of all. Know your weakness, work on them, evaluate yourself constantly and turn them into strengths.

When Michael first came into the NBA league, his critics pegged him as just a slasher and a dunker who could not shoot from the outside. Michael took that criticism and focused his efforts on improving his shot. He worked on it so much that his shot became another weapon in his arsenal and it made him even more dangerous on court. Then his critics picked on another aspect of his game. They said he could not defend well. He again took this very positively. He worked on his defensive skills so much that he even won the NBA defensive player of the year award. During a television interview, James Jordan, Michael Jordan's late father, said that what Michael had was a competition problem. The person he tries to outdo most of the time was himself.

Michael became so good at his game because of always working and improving on his weakness that he led the Chicago Bulls to six NBA titles and along the way he won five regular season MVP (most valuable player) titles and three all star MVP titles. Michael's prowess as a basketball player, his fame, transcended the basketball court; he became such a brand that he got a lot of endorsement deals from companies such as Nike. Because of the endorsements Michael Jordan became the first billion dollar athlete in the world.

"When I can't find a way to do anything, I will find a way to do it."

One of his most famous quotes is; "When I can't find a way to do anything, I will find a way to do it."

Identify your areas of weakness. Start working on them and soon they will be strengths. The time to start is now!

#8

IDENTIFYING YOUR GOALS AND SETTLING FOR NOTHING LESS

What do you want out of life? Are you the type of person who takes whatever comes your way and you are okay with it? Do you know that success does not come to you; you go to it? I am a strong believer that, "Life does not pay you what you deserve; it pays you what you negotiate with it."

In life there are three kinds of people. (1)*There are those who make things happen* (2) *There are those who watch things happen and;* (3) *there are those who wonder what happened.*

Which category are you in?

"Life does not pay you what you deserve; it pays you what you negotiate with it."

I just love the story of Jacob in the Bible. Jacob was certainly not one to sit back and watch things happen and then wonder what happened. He certainly belonged to the category of those who made things happen. His story of how he connived with his mother to steal his brother Essau's birth right by cheating his father that he was actually Essau while not being the most inspiring tells you of a man who was a go getter at whatever cost. It tells you of a man who constantly asked himself, if others could get, "why not me?" Jacob started his struggles for what he wanted right in his mother's womb. He was the twin brother of Essau and according to their mother Rebecca the two were always struggling against each other in her womb. She even asked the Lord why something like that should happen and the Lord told her, "Two nations are within you, you will give birth to two rival peoples. One will be stronger than the other, the elder will serve the younger." Jacob was the younger and was born tightly holding the heel of Essau. It was as if he was asking why Essau wanted to leave him behind in the womb. He understood the blessings that came with being the first born. He forced Essau to give him his rights as the first born in exchange of a meal one day when Essau came home from hunting and he was very hungry. Essau agreed. Jacob did not stop there. With the help of his mother who clearly loved him more than she loved Essau, he succeeded in conning his blind father Isaac into blessing him by pretending to be Essau. When Essau discovered what had happened he plotted to kill Jacob but the mother knew about it and advised Jacob to take off to his uncle Laban. It was a while there that Jacob saw and fell in love with Laban's younger daughter Rachel. He made it known to him that he wanted to marry Rachel and He told him he had to work for him for seven years before he could marry her. Jacob agreed, after seven years, Laban tricked him and brought him the older daughter Leah at night. When he confronted Laban in the morning, he told him he was only following tradition where the younger daughter could not be married off before the older one. Jacob loved Rachel so much he opted to also marry Rachel and work for another seven years for Laban. He clearly knew what he wanted and he was not one to give up easily. He had to make things happen his way no matter what. That is patience! It is said good things come to those who wait. How many of us have that kind of patience? I think that kind of patience can only be practised by someone who clearly knows what he wants and knows how to get it.

good things come to those who wait.

The story of Jacob that impresses me the most is when he wrestled with an angel a Penile the whole night. When the angel realised it was nearing day break, he pleaded with Jacob to let him go but Jacob said he would not let him go until he blessed him. The angel told him he had wrestled with God and with men, and he had won, he blessed him and his name would no longer be Jacob but Israel.

I saw a post from someone on face book which summed up Jacob; "I know what I want, where I can get it, how I can get it and what I will do with it once I get it." What about you?

Jacob was simply a go getter. He identified what he wanted and would not settle for anything less. His story resonates very well with something that happened to me when I sat my standard seven exams. As is tradition in our country, when you are about to set your end of primary school exams, you select the schools you would like to join for high school education. I was so clear in my mind that I wanted to join Alliance High school that I put all my four choices as (1) Alliance High School (2) Alliance High School (3) Alliance High School (4) Alliance High School.

"I know what I want, where I can get it, how I can get it and what I will do with it once I get it."

I truly believed in my ability and I did not want to take chances with my choices. For it was either Alliance High School or Alliance High School. When we did the exams I was so sure I was going to make the cut for Alliance High School. I had a good feeling about it. When the results came out I had scored the highest marks that were available on offer which made me feel that all what remained was the admission letter to Alliance. Shock on me! When the letter eventually came it was not from Alliance. It was from Njiiri High School. I could not understand since I had not selected any other school and I had made the cut for Alliance. I was devastated. I never quite understood what happened but my suspicion to date is that someone influential in the primary school changed my choices. Perhaps for fear that nobody had ever dreamt of going to Alliance High School leave alone actually going there. That was mainly because nobody had scored maximum points before then. Those were stories only read in newspapers from other places.

My parents and elder siblings convinced me that Njiiri High School was a good school. My interest was not to go to a good school but to a great school!

They however convinced me to join the school and work hard. I accepted but I made it my primary goal to work extremely hard to make it to Alliance high school for form five and six. At least I knew there was another chance unlike nowadays when after form four the next level is university or just college. My brother, Charles, offered to pay my school fees and I will forever be grateful for his kindness and generosity. However he had his own family which also had its own needs. Sometimes fees would be delayed and I would be sent home for weeks. But this never made me lose sight of my goal. I was so determined to make it to Alliance High School that I used to carry my books home every time I was sent away so that I could study. In form 1 and 2 I was sort of going through a High school culture shock. So many experiences were a first for me. It was my first time to wear shoes, my first time to wear long trousers, my first time to use a shower; at home I used to bathe in the river, my first time to see a student brought to school in a limousine, my first time to live in an area with near temperate climate. All these firsts took time to sink in and they affected my academic performance. I was in the bottom half of the top ten in my class and I knew my chances of joining Alliance were very slim unless I pulled up my socks. Alliance had only few slots for students from other schools in form five. When I got to form three, I knew something had to change. I knew I had to get into the top five in class if I stood any chance of going to Alliance in form five. Luckily we had done subject selection and I had dropped the art subjects which I felt were dragging me down. I was more of the science kind of a student. By the time I went to form four I had worked so hard that I had broken into the top three. But I was still not comfortable. I had to be sure and the only way to be sure was to be number 2 or 1. I doubled my efforts. I made teachers my friends and I constantly consulted them. This was made easy for me by the fact that I was a class prefect. When we did our mocks examination, I became number 2. During the following holidays, I talked to one of my mentors who advised me that positions were not enough. My aim should be to get very good grades. I started working to get the best grades on offer. I knew if I got the grades, nobody would change my choices and therefore Alliance would have no choice this time round but to admit me. In the month just before sitting the final exams, there was a national tradition in schools where students would write in other students' autograph books inspirational messages to motivate them for exams and in the life after. The best quote I got was from one of my best friends in class, Robert. He wrote; "The worthiest ambition of a man is the pursuit of excellence." He continued to add; *"I know you have been working hard to go to Alliance and I know you will make it."* That was the best message I got. It was the fuel I needed for the remaining part of school before exams. When I sat the exams, I felt so sure that I had done my very best and all I had to do was to wait for the results and for Alliance to admit me to form five. It came as no surprise to me when I tied with my friend in top position in the school and we were both admitted to Alliance High School for form five and six. What I could not get in form one I got in form five, the High School of my dreams. Besides making it to Alliance High School for advanced studies, my performance in Njiiri High School taught me a very vital lesson in life; "That places do not make people, people make places."

"That places do not make people, people make places."

When you identify what you want in life, focus your energies and work constantly towards it. Always remember, according to Ralph Waldo Emerson; "The world makes way for the man who knows where he is going and in the process, even helping him get there."

"The world makes way for the man who knows where he is going and in the process, even helping him get there."

-RALPH WALDO EMERSON

In the Bible, there is an interesting story of a tax collector called Zaccheus. One day Jesus was passing by and Zaccheus really wanted to see him but he was a very short man, he realized that in the middle of the multitude of people he stood no chance. This however did not deter him. His desire drove him to become very innovative. He decided to climb a tree. His efforts did not only afford him the chance to see but Jesus actually noticed him, called him and invited him to follow him.

Chuck Danes, the founder of Enlightened Journey Enterprises says; *"Everything you want is out there waiting for you to receive it, but it is going to take transforming want to a deep rooted desire for you to receive it."* That is what Zaccheus did! *What do you want? What is your tree?*

Become a Zaccheus today!

#9

TIME, PLANNING AND PAYING ATTENTION TO DETAIL

Do you take time to plan your day, work, relations with God, relationship with people? Do you have a plan for your life? How much attention to detail do you pay in the things you do? Given another chance, what would you do differently and how?

The second last flash I saw was of me as a boy enjoying every moment of life including courageously and happily fighting off a life threatening illness. It then changed on me as an adult. always rushing through things and never stopping to enjoy life. This flash bothered me the most and when I woke up it was the most vivid in my mind. I realized that it was a clear message about how I was managing my life. I realized this accident did not just happen, it happened for a purpose. It happened that I could get a chance to reflect on my life, to learn that life was to be enjoyed not endured. I realized I had stopped living my life and I was just going through it in a haphazard manner, chasing after business but never stopping to enjoy life.

When you think about life, isn't the nicest thing that happens to you everyday just waking up healthy? Do you ever pause to thank God for giving you a new day, air to breathe, food to eat, a roof over your head, sunshine, rain and all the beautiful things of life or are you the kind of person who just whine about everything?

What do you do with your day? Do you maximize on the 24 hrs which everyone gets indiscriminately? Or do you just while them away and just watch others put their time into good use, prosper and get blessed in front of your own eyes and wonder what happened to you? I just love what televangelist, Bishop T.D Jakes says; "Every new day is God's gift to you, what you do with it is your gift to God." What you give back to God he multiplies it for you according to your efforts.

A lot of people do not realize that in life every new day is an investment opportunity, investment in your relationship with God, in your health, in your relationships with people, in your work, all of which translate to your happiness. If you don't take advantage of it you will always be a spectator as others continue to thrive in business, excel in school, excel in sports and generally live a more fulfilled happier, healthier and wealthier life. Happiness is not a destination, it is a journey.

Happiness is not a destination, it is a journey.

If you have been watching others progress while you stagnate it is time to have a serious conversation with yourself. Call yourself to an immediate meeting and let the agenda be; 'why not me?' Do not leave that meeting without the answers. Do not leave that meeting without a plan of action. Do not leave that meeting without a binding resolution to follow through your plan of action. *Remember* ***good minds plan, but great minds execute*****!**

Consider including the following in your plan of action:

i) Setting goals everyday.
ii) Executing those goals.
iii) Evaluating those goals at the end of the day.
iv) Setting bigger and better goals the next day.
v) Executing them.
vi) Evaluating them at the end of the day.

To be successful in anything, one has to continually improve. Winston Churchill once said; *"To improve is to change, to be perfect is to change continually"* Do not be afraid to change. It is the only way to be better. After all, the only constant thing in this world is change itself.

To be successful in anything, one has to continually improve.

Robin Sharma in his book, 'Extra ordinary' describes the hour between 5 am-6 am as a holy hour and he divides it into 4 sections;

i) First 15 minutes: - wake up and pray.
ii) Second 15 minutes: - Read something to inspire you for the day.
iii) Third 15 minutes: - do some physical exercise.
iv) Last 15 minutes: - Plan your day and write down your plans for the day.

Robin Sharma says, for this process to be engrained in your system, you must practice it everyday for at least 21 days. Then it becomes a habit. What becomes a habit eventually becomes character. What becomes character defines your destiny.

Always remember everything starts with a thought. Thoughts are processed in your mind. That is why it is absolutely important to irrigate your mind with positivity and with the right attitude. Whatever your mind conceives you can achieve. A lot of people conceive great ideas but they never actualize those ideas. Why? The reason most people do not actualize the ideas is because they do not take time to put down their ideas on paper and therefore they don't have any reference point. It is so easy to forget things which are not written down because there is no commitment to them. When you write things down you make a commitment to them. It is easy to execute things you are committed to. Things that are written down are easier to review, evaluate and improve and finally execute. Just like the bible says in Habakkuk 2:2 says, write down your vision in bold letters. After

What becomes a habit eventually becomes character. What becomes character defines your destiny.

writing down your ideas it is important to share the same with people you respect especially your mentors. These kinds of people will help you achieve your dreams by continually reminding you that you committed yourself to them. They also help you by continually wanting to know how far you have gone in your journey to achieving your dream. These kinds of people can also help you with ideas to improve and fast track on your goals. If you want to enjoy your life, structure your life. Write down what you want to do with your time, with your money, with your relationships and constantly evaluate the progress on the same. But always remember to peg a time frame to your dream. Napoleon Hill says; "A dream is a goal with a deadline."

I recently attended a leadership seminar conducted by professor Embeywa. He summarized concepts of how to do self-evaluation into two laws:

i) WHYA – What Have You Achieved?
ii) WHYB – What Have You Become?

Having practiced architecture for the last 20 years, I understand perfectly the absolute importance of putting your dreams down on paper. When a client comes to me they have these beautiful ideas about the kind of house they want but the ideas are just usually in their minds. My duty is first and foremost to write down a project brief capturing all their ideas. Once we all agree that the brief is a true reflection of their dreams, I proceed to prepare a conceptual design. This helps us brainstorm further with the client and they are able to see whether their ideas have been adequately captured in the conceptual design. If not, we agree on what needs to be changed. When we all agree that the conceptual design is okay, I proceed to prepare the final drawings, with plans showing the agreed space dispositions, dimensions and also impressions of how the structure will look like. This becomes the working document for implementation of the project. It also means any amendments will be done within the general context of the document. This ensures that even if any one of the parties is not present, the reference is always there and the dream lives on. That is the beauty of putting down your dreams on paper. Dreams should live on even long after the dreamer is gone. That is how a dream becomes a legacy.

If you want to build a legacy you must invest time and you must pay a lot of attention to detail

We all know that Christianity exists and continues to grow because Jesus dream of salvation for mankind was well documented in the Bible. I believe if no one bothered to write down the biblical scriptures for posterity, perhaps Christianity would not exist. The same can be said about Islam and all other religions.

Nothing great has ever happened overnight or by chance. Every great thing takes time to build. If you want to be celebrated, take time to build your legacy. It is said that it takes 17 hours to assemble a Toyota but it takes 6 months to build a Rolls Royce. A Toyota is machine assembled but a Rolls Royce is hand made. That is why it takes much longer to build the Rolls Royce because of attention to detail. Every single thing in the Rolls Royce is done by hand! No wonder the cheapest Rolls Royce costs about US dollars 200,000 while you can get a brand new Toyota for as little as US dollars 14,000.

Nothing great has ever happened overnight or by chance.

If you want to build a legacy you must invest time and you must pay a lot of attention to detail because as they say, the devil is in the detail. If you think about the most eye catching structures ever built, they took much longer time to be completed than their contemporary structures. Because so much time was spent on them, there was so much attention to detail they stood out and became the stuff of legend. To sample but a few, the Great Wall of China took 2,000 years to build and no wonder it was called great! It is the structure that took the longest period to build in recorded history. There were other buildings of note that took long to construct because of the attention to detail like: The coliseum which was a glorious symbol of ancient Rome. It took 10 years to build and it became a well-known Roman landmark. Built between A.D 70 and A.D 80, it could hold up to 80,000 people which is at par with many modern stadiums. Looking at the Coliseum there is no doubt that Romans were unrivalled at their time for their advanced engineering abilities and architectural skills. One marvels at the way they were able to construct such complex elements as arches, tunnels below the arena and even hydraulic mechanisms way before the advent of construction cranes and other modern construction equipment. This was only possible because they invested time. They used their hands and paid a lot of attention to detail and they were able to achieve a legendary structure.

We can speak about other outstanding structures like the Parthenon, the great pyramid of Giza and many more structures that took long to build and became landmarks, but the one that stands out most for me is the Taj Mahal. Taj Mahal stands at the heart of India and it is to me perhaps the perfect example of meticulous planning, paying attention to detail and taking time to build a legacy.

The construction of the Taj Mahal was commissioned by the emperor of Mughal (an Indian kingdom then), Shah Jahan as a tribute of love to his late wife Mumtaz Mahal who had died giving birth to their 14th child. The extra-ordinary edifice was commissioned in 1632 and it took 22 years to complete and some 22,000 laborers. Because it was a tribute of love, Jahan left nothing to chance; from the design to the way it was built, everything was meticulously planned and executed. The building is clad with white marble, painstakingly sourced. This legendary building is so amazingly beautiful that it is considered one of the Seven Wonders of the World. Believe it or not it attracts between 2 to 4 million tourists every year! Compare that for a single building with half a million tourists who visit Kenya annually with all her natural splendor. An English poet, Sir Edwin Arnold described it as; *"Not a piece of Architecture as other buildings are, but the proud passion of an emperor's love wrought in living stone."*

How was the story of the Taj Mahal possible? Jahan knew that to achieve anything great you must invest time, time to plan and time to execute. He knew if you love what you are doing and you want to leave a legacy you must be willing and ready to pay the price of attention to detail. Greatness has no shortcuts. The story of the Taj Mahal has been melting the hearts of listeners since the time it became visible, some 352 years ago. It is considered a living example of eternal love.

to achieve anything great you must invest time, time to plan and time to execute.

What is your story?

Are you investing time in writing your story?

Are you paying attention to detail?

Is your story a tribute of love to something or someone?

"Greatness is a result of a labor of love." Steve Muiru

#10

THE MOST IMPORTANT LESSONLEARN, EARN, GIVE BACK

"The meaning of life is to find your gift; the purpose of it is to give it away."

PABLO PICASSO

Do you invest in People? If you were to die today; what would people eulogize you for? Are there things you wish you had done for others that you haven't done?

> *"The greatness of a man is not in how much wealth he acquires but in his integrity and his ability to affect those around him positively."*
>
> **-BOB MARLEY**

The last flash I saw was about community projects I have been involved in. This flash was very significant to me because there are things I am doing now and really loving it. I had resisted doing some and did others half heartedly before the accident. I have come to understand perfectly through my own experience that as Bob Marley one said; "The greatness of a man is not in how much wealth he acquires but in his integrity and his ability to affect those around him positively."

I remember in 2006, a friend of mine who had just been promoted as a principal of a school in a rural area in Murang'a County; came to me and requested me to join his school board of management. I out rightly refused and I thought I had good reasons for it. Number 1, the school was in my view too far away from my office. The road to the school was not good at all so I could not see myself driving there every so often and wrecking my car. After all nobody was going to pay me for it and the sitting allowance would not be enough to take care of the wear and tire, leave alone my time. Number 2, I felt I had no connection with the school whatsoever because I am not from that area. I had never been there and I didn't know anyone in that school except the principal. This gentleman is not the kind to give up easily. He kept on coming back to my office to ask me the same thing over and over again. On the tenth visit he really looked desperate. I decided to ask him why he was so keen on me joining his board. We had worked with him on some small projects in Mang'u High School and he told me that during that period, he had identified some leadership qualities in me that he wanted to bring on board in his new school management team. The new board was to be formed the following year. I still refused and he left looking very dejected. I thought that matter was over and done with. Two months later the same gentleman came to my office with a white envelop bearing my name on it. Without many explanations, he handed me the envelope and told me to open and read. It was an appointment letter as member of the school board from the Minister of Education and the last part was a request to give a written and duly signed acceptance of the appointment to be forwarded to the minister's office. I looked at this gentleman and he said to me; "Let me know whether you really value our friendship by how you respond to that letter." I just couldn't turn him down after all his efforts, so I decided to play along but I was so clear in my mind that I was just going to play a peripheral role in the board. He invited me for the inauguration of the board which was to take place the following week. He also explained to me that, elections of the office bearers were to be held on the same day. He wanted me to take up the position of chairman of procurement committee. I just listened and said nothing.

On the material day, I refused to go and I switched off my phone. I knew there was no way I would be elected as an office bearer in absentia. I also knew he could not propose my name to people who did not know me. My plan worked perfectly, or so I thought. I was later to learn the elections were done, the board was inaugurated and I was "safe" from any responsibilities in the board.

The next board meeting happened to be just after the release of the 2007 Kenya certificate of secondary school exam results and we were to go and discuss the results and chart a way forward for our school. The results were not very good and the local Member of Parliament, Mr. Peter Kenneth was in attendance to drive home the message that the school was not doing well and something had to happen to change the trend. He said this without mincing words. I remember telling him that he should not hold us responsible for the results as we had just taken over as a board and that the results were the responsibility of the previous board.

That did not sit well with the MP. He quickly reminded me that once you take up an office you have to bear all its responsibilities from day one. He also quoted Winston Churchill and said; "The price of greatness is responsibility." He finished off his reprimand by saying, unless we wanted to continue with mediocrity we should take responsibility of the performance. I don't like being associated with failure. I told members that we had to immediately form an academic committee to look into the academic affairs of the school. Everybody agreed but since there had never been such a committee in the school, they all mandated me with the responsibility of composing it and chairing it. The responsibilities I was running away from started catching up with me.

> *"The price of greatness is responsibility."*
>
> -WINSTON CHURCHILL

This was to be the beginning of a long chapter of my service to the school. The academic committee came up with many recommendations but a lot of them could not be implemented immediately because of lack of resources. However, we tried our best. The following year, after the release of KSCE results again as usual we had a board meeting to discuss the school's performance. Unfortunately we had not performed well. The area Member of Parliament was in attendance again. This time his agenda was different. Immediately the meeting was called to order, he rose to move a motion of having the sitting board chairman step down. He argued that, since the chairman had national political interests and he seemed not to have much time to manage the affairs of the school. According to the MP, that is why the school was not performing well. The chairman did not agree with him at all and a fierce argument ensued. We spent four good hours discussing the fate of the chairman. I was getting very uncomfortable with the proceedings and I honestly felt we were wasting time on a non-issue instead of discussing the agenda for the day. I raised my hand and requested to make a contribution. When I stood to talk for some reason everyone kept quiet and listened. My contribution was very brief and to the point. I simply addressed the chairman directly and told him that since as he had rightly pointed out, being on the board was purely a voluntary service and the chairman's position was an honor bestowed on him by the members, then he should at least be humble enough to step aside for the day and allow members to deliberate on the agenda for the day and at the end of the meeting members would decide whether to retain him or get someone else to be their chairman. Up to date I am not sure whether it is what I said or how I said, because the chairman without any further argument agreed to allow someone else to chair the session for the day. He was nevertheless very categorical that he was doing it not because he was wrong, but because of the respect he had for me. I did not know what I got myself into. It was as if the MP had been silently praying and waiting for that moment. He immediately stood up and told the members; "I do not know why you grope in the darkness for leadership while you have natural leaders amongst you. It has taken Mr. Muiru five minutes to resolve what we have been trying to resolve for four hours. Kindly let him be your chairman for today's meeting. Then you can decide what to do with the position at the end of the meeting." That was the last thing I wanted to do. I thought I was just trying to bring sanity to the meeting by addressing the chairman directly but I did not expect this turn of events. He beckoned me to move over to the chairman's seat which was now vacant. Eventually I took the chairman's seat and at that point the MP left us to continue with the meeting. He had that look of 'mission accomplished.'

Time was not on our side, immediately I took charge of the meeting, I was very clear in my mind that we were only going to discuss the school's academic performance and the other three items on the agenda paper would have to wait until the next board meeting. That is what I told members and nobody raised an objection. I made the meeting very interactive by engaging members with questions and allowing them to air whatever view they held about the way forward with the academic performance. At the end of the meeting I took advantage of being on the chair and gave a detailed outline of the plans I thought would work to improve our school academically. I could tell I had established a serious connection with the members just by observing their reactions every time I made a point.

When it was time for AOB, I decided to give everybody a chance to give theirs so that even the shy ones who ordinarily would not raise their hands to contribute would have no excuse not to say their bit. Everything I did that day seemed to work against my earlier held position of not wanting a leadership position in the school. All the members including the chairman said that I had conducted the meeting so well that they wanted me to be their chairman. The sponsor though had an issue; I am not Catholic and the school is Catholic sponsored. The Catholic Church has a policy that all the schools they sponsor have to be chaired by a Catholic. When the local priest raised the issue I was very happy because I knew I had gotten my escape route or so I thought. What happened next reminded me of the biblical Jonah story. Despite his refusal to go to Nineveh, God used the most unorthodox method to get him there. And so it was to happen for me as well. The diocesan education secretary who is basically the Catholic Church education overseer and therefore senior to the local priest, was in attendance. He overruled the priest. He said as long I was a committed Christian he had no issue with me being chairman of the board. He even proceeded to say that he felt I had demonstrated more commitment to the school during the meeting than many catholic chairmen he had encountered. With that he gave his endorsement and that is how I became chairman of the board of governors of Ithanga secondary school.

That was a big life lesson for me. When God wants you to do something, no matter how much you want to run away from it, it will catch up with you. A lot of people are running away from their destinies because they have not discovered what their destinies are. I was lucky mine was revealed to me in a very divine way. It could not have been anything else. The signs were all there that God sent me there to make a change. I was the only member of the board who had no history with the school or the immediate neighborhood. Indeed I remember Mr. Peter Kenneth once introducing me to some friends of his as the agent of change in the school which would later turn prophetic.

Before my first official full board meeting as the chairman, I decided to engage all the stake holders and listen to their issues. I listened to my fellow members of the board, to students, to teachers and to parents. I knew if I stood a chance to make a difference in that school, I had to listen to all the stake holders in order to understand their fears, their aspirations and their expectations. It is former American President, Woodrow Wilson who said; "The ear of a leader must ring with the voice of the people."

> *"The ear of a leader must ring with the voice of the people."*
>
> -WOODROW WILSON

Finally I sat with the principal and together we compiled a list of all the challenges the school faced. Needless to say the challenges were many. First of all, the school is a mixed school. Secondly, all the boys are day scholars. Thirdly, some girls are day scholars while others board. This is like having three schools in one. One of the biggest challenges was discipline and of course discipline affects performance. We had to deal with this as a matter of urgency. I then came up with a ten point agenda of infrastructural projects and programs which I felt would help uplift the school in all spheres. As I write this book we have achieved nine of them and only one is remaining but I am confident it will also be accomplished in the next one year, God being our helper. That project is building teachers houses. Some of the key projects have been: 1. Building and equipping a school library. 2. Building four new class rooms to allow for expansion of the school from a two stream to a three stream. 3. Building modern water borne toilets to replace the pit latrines. 4. Buying a school bus. 5. Establishing and equipping a computer laboratory for the school among others. All these interventions coupled with consistent motivational talks to the students and teachers have helped create a desirable identity for the school which was lacking before. We have also been able to consistently set and achieve our academic targets every year. What really inspires me to keep going in this school is that they have consistently been increasing the numbers qualifying for university admission. In a day school like this and being in a hardship area achieving this milestone is quite an achievement. The school has also won the Equity bank wings to fly scholarship, which goes to the best student in KCSE in a region, for the last four years which is no mean feat.

Whenever I reflect on my journey and what we have achieved during that period, I feel extremely humbled. I know without any fear of contradiction that some of my best moments in life have been defined by my service to this school. Just seeing students who initially could not express themselves confidently and in correct grammar not only participating but also winning national essay writing competitions is simply a miracle. Walking into a bank and a former student of the school courteously gives you first class service and tells you that you inspired him to succeed, brings tears of joy to my eyes. I have learnt that giving back to society is one of the most fulfilling callings in life. John C Maxwell, a leadership coach guru says; "You have not truly lived if you have not done something for someone who can never pay you back."

"You have not truly lived if you have not done something for someone who can never pay you back."

-JOHN C MAXWELL

In 1889, millionaire industrialist, Andrew Carnegie wrote an essay called

'*Gospel of Wealth.*' In it he said that the life of a wealthy person should have two periods: a time for acquiring it and a time for redistributing it. I would like to restate this and say that the life of a modern person should have three stages: Learn, Earn and Give back. Luckily all the stages can and indeed should coexist. If you are wondering why you are being *tolerated* instead of being *celebrated,* may be you have never known the secret, start giving back to society. You can give back your ideas, your service, your resources, whatever you can. You will certainly be celebrated.

You do not have to ask "Why Not Me?" Be a people person. MAKE IT YOU!

#11

OVERCOMING YOUR FEARS

"Too many of us are not living our dreams because we are living are fears."

LES BROWN.

What are your fears? Do you fear venturing into the unknown? Do you hold back from falling in love because of fear of being hurt? Do you hold back from starting a business because of fear of failure?

As human beings we have a lot of fear. Fear of the unknown. Most people fail to reach their full potential simply because they fear venturing beyond their comfort zone. A lot of people like to remain with the status quo. Unfortunately nobody ever crossed the ocean by remaining on the shores! If you want to cross the ocean, you must be prepared to lose sight of the shores. If you want to start a business, you should be prepared to take a risk. Without risk there can never be progress! Everything great that has ever been achieved was made possible by someone who took a risk to do it. Deciding to take the risk however, does not guarantee instant success. It is nevertheless the most critical step in overcoming ones fears.

If you want to cross the ocean, you must be prepared to lose sight of the shores... Everything great that has ever been achieved was made possible by someone who took a risk to do it.

If Thomas Edison had not decided to take the risk with his experiment for coming up with an electric light bulb, perhaps we would still be in darkness. If the Wright brothers had not taken the risk to design and fly a crude plane, perhaps we would never have seen and experienced the luxury of a concord. If Graham Bell had not ventured into telephony, perhaps we would not be enjoying the cell phones of today. Did these guys succeed at the first time of asking? Of course not! Thomas Edison failed in his experiment over

1000 times. What was common with all of them? They identified what they wanted and overcame the fear of failure!

For us to hope for tomorrow, we must embrace today and overcome the fear of what tomorrow holds.

Life itself is a risk. When you were born nobody knew whether you would live or die. You lived! Others were not as lucky. Since then you have gone through life every day not knowing what tomorrow holds for you. Nobody has ever seen 'tomorrow' because we can only live today and hope for tomorrow. For us to hope for tomorrow, we must embrace today and overcome the fear of what tomorrow holds. Tomorrow is never really in our hands. This is very important to understand because most fears are born out of not being sure of the outcome of something.

In love relationships, some people hold back their true feelings for the same fear. They feel if they let go fully, they risk getting a heart break. The truth is; you can never really enjoy a love relationship unless and until you commit yourself fully to the other person. I am not a relationship expert but I can say this for free, most people I have talked to, have confessed to have only truly enjoyed being in relationships where there was true friendship between them. If you have been wondering why you are always a maid of honor but never the bride, perhaps you need to deal with the fear of a heart break. Perhaps you need to invest in the risk of creating genuine friendships with prospective partners. What values do you attach to a relationship? I love some lines I picked from the movie, 'Coming to America' by Eddie Murphy. He says; *"I would rather be with a lady who not only arouses my loins but also my intellect."*In the same movie he says; "No journey is too long when a man finds what he seeks." I am sure this would also apply the other way round. What do you go for in a relationship? What are you seeking for? Go for someone who makes you laugh, makes you smile, stimulates your mind and body, sings lullabies for you and keeps you awake with exciting bedtime stories. But above all, have faith in that person. A relationship can be the difference between success and failure!

Are you afraid of what others will say about what you are doing? This is another common fear for a lot of people. The process of thought is individual. The only thing that God gave you complete control over is your thoughts. If you are never worried about what others will think about your thoughts, why should you worry about what they will think about your actions? *If you can think it, you can do it!* Do not be a hostage of others. Everything great started with a thought from an individual. When you think of successful companies, they were all started by an individual; an individual who had overcome the fear of failure. Big companies may be run by boards of management but there is no such a thing as a collective thought. Anything other than an individual thought is a compromise. What are you thinking? Are you thinking big or are you thinking small? What you will achieve in life will be as big as your thinking. I like what Donald Trump says; "You are going to think anyway so why not think big." You are the sum total of your thoughts.

"You are going to think anyway so why not think big."

-DONALD TRUMP

Overcoming ones fears, thinking the right thoughts and putting those thoughts into action is a sure way of starting ones journey to greatness. That journey however, requires another key ingredient without which the journey may abort. That ingredient is called faith. Faith is a state of mind which might be called the 'mainspring of the soul' through which ones aims, desires and purposes may be translated into their physical or financial equivalent. Faith enables human beings to penetrate deeply into the secrets of Nature and to understand Nature's language. Dale Carnegie in his book; "The Master Key to

Faith is a state of mind which might be called the 'mainspring of the soul'

Riches", describes faith as a royal visitor which enters only the mind that has been set in order through self-discipline. He says; "In the fashion of all royalty, faith commands the best room – no, the finest suite – in the mental dwelling place. It will not be shunted into servants' quarters, and it will not associate with envy, greed, superstition, revenge, vanity, doubt or FEAR!

Getting the full significance of this truth will give you an understanding of this mysterious power that has baffled even scientists through the ages. For the power of faith to be really effective, one requires to form a mastermind alliance in his life. This must of necessity include having faith in the infinite intelligence (God). As they say; "Do your best and leave the rest to God."

I will not do justice to the power of faith without telling you a story. My dad is eighty nine years old. He has been battling cancer and cancer related complications for the last ten years. Through him, I have literally seen the power of applied faith at work. In 2005, he was diagnosed with cancer of the bladder which according to the doctors was already at level three. In short, it was advanced. Two urologists specialist said the only option he had was to have the bladder removed and be fitted with a catheter and an external urine bag for the rest of his life. I made a decision to seek further advice from other doctors. We eventually got a doctor who performed a cystoscopy on him.

After a month of radiotherapy, dad was discharged to continue with clinics from home. The doctor said there were no guarantees, after six months of clinics, my dad was declared cancer free. The doctor said that was nothing short of a miracle. While this surprised the doctor my dad said he had never lost faith in God. He always believed he had many more years to live. In 2014, he was diagnosed with prostate cancer. The doctor who had operated him previously said it was totally unrelated to the first cancer. He gave us hope, if dad would agree to go through a minor surgical procedure (ocidectomy) the advancement of the cancer would be slowed and he would be able to live a normal life. Dad had no objection. The operation was done and he was discharged to continue with his medication at home. There is a famous saying that "When it rains it pours". Trouble sometimes comes with relatives.

"When it rains it pours".

Two months after being discharged from hospital, dad fell and broke his right thigh bone. He was back in hospital on traction for two months before he had completely healed from the operation. This set back took quite a toll on him. It has been a real battle for the last one year. I remember in July last year, dad was so sick he could not eat or drink anything. He had to depend entirely on hospital drip. The nurses had put a big red sticker by his bedside indicating "Nil by Mouth!" He has been my best friend, looking at him on the hospital bed was too much for me to bear. He was a pale shadow of the vibrant man I knew. I remember posting on my face book page that; "May thy will be done." It was as if I was saying good bye.

While I was busy worrying about him, dad had other ideas; I visited him one day and he shocked me. There was a patient on the bed next to his who was screaming in pain. Dad beckoned on me to draw closer. He wanted to whisper something to me because he could not speak loudly. He told me to pray for the screaming patient for he was in real pain. I looked at dad and asked him; "you are in real pain, you have not eaten for a week, you are in bad shape, how can you be thinking of the pain of others?" He mustered enough strength and told me; "Steve when you have faith in God, everything is okay and you are at peace."

Dad is now back at home looking his old vibrant self and walking around using a walking stick. In early December, 2015 he managed to go to church to witness his best friends' 60th wedding anniversary.

What better way to conclude my book than to share the wisdom I got from my dad. After being on this earth for eighty nine years, he surely has earned the right to say it; "Have faith In God."

Faith can move mountains. Faith will remove obstacles from your way. Faith will help you overcome your fears.

Faith can move mountains. Faith will remove obstacles from your way. Faith will help you overcome your fears.

Faith will transform you from a Victim to a Victor! Faith will move you from *'just being among the others to being the one!'*

www.ingramcontent.com/pod-product-compliance
Lightning Source LLC
LaVergne TN
LVHW050600160826
845677LV00011B/2399

* 9 7 8 9 9 6 6 7 9 0 4 6 0 *